MEL BAY PRESENTS

Sacred Violin Solos

BY BURTON ISAAC

CONTENTS

AMAZING GRACE

Piano

Early American Melody

FAITH OF OUR FATHERS

Henri F. Hemy
1818–1888

6

LET US BREAK BREAD TOGETHER

American Folk Hymn

9

10

O FOR A THOUSAND TONGUES TO SING

Carl G. Gläser
1784-1829

CHRISTMAS MEDLEY

Arr. B. H. Isaac

O Come All Ye Faithful

O Little Town of Bethlehem

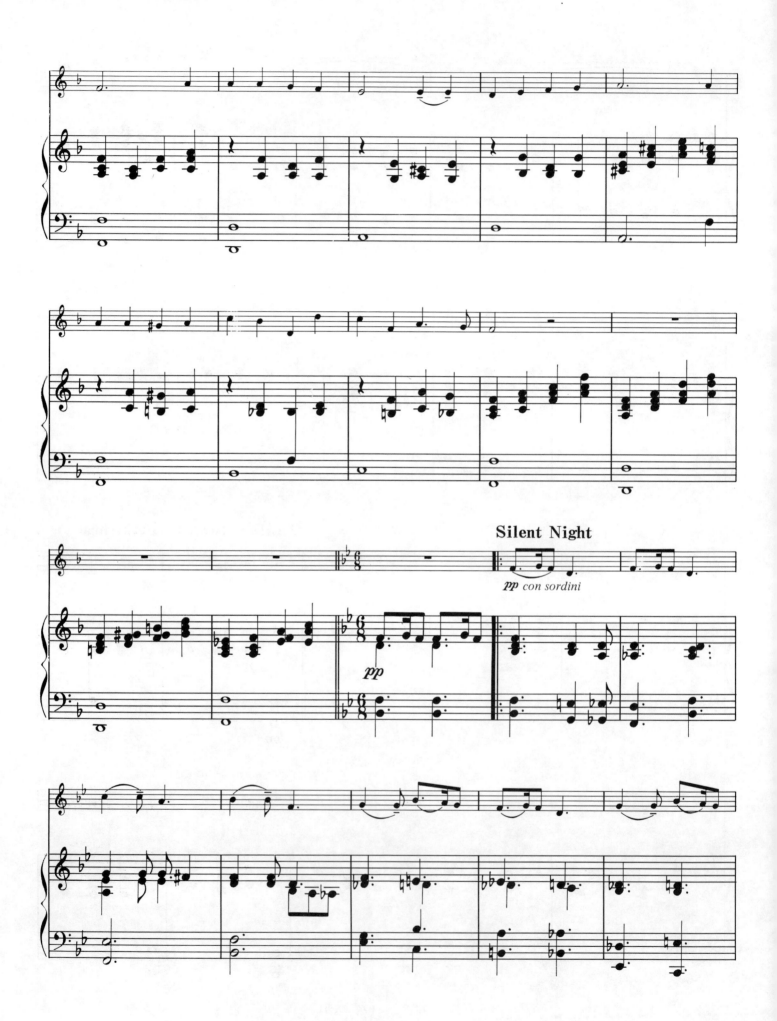

Silent Night

pp con sordini

18

Joy to the World

COME THOU LONG EXPECTED JESUS

Rowland H. Prichard 1811 87

24

WERE YOU THERE

American Folk Hymn

26

segue

O SACRED HEAD

Hans Hassler
J.S. Bach

JESU, JOY OF MAN'S DESIRING

J.S. Bach

JESUS SHALL REIGN

John Hatton d. 1973

FAIREST LORD JESUS

Piano

Crusader's Hymn 17th cent.

"Music for the
Church Triumphant"